AHEARN SCHOPFER AND ASSOCIATES ■ ARBOR SOUTH ARCHITECTURE ■ AWKS-ARCHITECTS WELLS KASTNER SCHIPPER

BARGANIER DAVIS SIMS ARCHITECTS ASSOCIATED ■ BARRY FOX ASSOCIATES ARCHITECTS ■ BENVENUTI AND STEIN

BLACK + WHITE STUDIO ARCHITECTS ■ BOGGS & PARTNERS ARCHITECTS ■ BORIS BARANOVICH ARCHITECTS ■ BRIDGES

MARSH AND CARMO ■ BRIGGS ARCHITECTURE + DESIGN ■ CHRISTOPHER ROSE ARCHITECTS ■ COLLINS ARCHITECTS &

CONSTRUCTION ■ DESROSIERS ARCHITECTS ■ ELLIS NUNN & ASSOCIATES ■ ISLAND ARCHITECTS ■ JOHN MORRIS

ARCHITECTS ■ JSA ARCHITECTS   KRANNITZ GEHL ARCHITECTS

LEWIS GRAEBER III & ASSOCIATES   LLOYD & ASSOCIATES ARCHITECTS

LOCATI ARCHITECTS ■ LOONEY RICKS KISS ARCHITECTS ■ MCCORMACK + ETTEN ARCHITECTS ■ MCLAUGHLIN & ASSOCIATES

ARCHITECTS ■ MRJ ARCHITECTS ■ OUTERBRIDGE MORGAN ARCHITECTURE & SPACE PLANNING ■ PFVS-PORTMAN

FRUCHTMAN VINSON SUNDERLAND ARCHITECTS ■ RICHARD M. COLE & ASSOCIATES ARCHITECTS ■ ROBINETTE ARCHITECTS

ROGER BARTELS ARCHITECTS ■ RUDI FISHER ARCHITECTS ■ SCHEURER ARCHITECTS ■ SHAMBURGER DESIGN STUDIO ■ SMUCKLER

ARCHITECTS ■ SPENCER ARCHITECTS ■ STEVEN R. GRAVES ARCHITECTS ■ TMS ARCHITECTS ■ WEST CARROLL ARCHITECTURE

AHEARN SCHOPFER AND ASSOCIATES ■ ARBOR SOUTH ARCHITECTURE ■ AWKS-ARCHITECTS WELLS KASTNER SCHIPPER

BARGANIER DAVIS SIMS ARCHITECTS ASSOCIATED ■ BARRY FOX ASSOCIATES ARCHITECTS ■ BENVENUTI AND STEIN

BLACK + WHITE STUDIO ARCHITECTS ■ BOGGS & PARTNERS ARCHITECTS ■ BORIS BARANOVICH ARCHITECTS ■ BRIDGES

MARSH AND CARMO ■ BRIGGS ARCHITECTURE + DESIGN ■ CHRISTOPHER ROSE ARCHITECTS ■ COLLINS ARCHITECTS &

CONSTRUCTION ■ DESROSIERS ARCHITECTS ■ ELLIS NUNN & ASSOCIATES ■ ISLAND ARCHITECTS ■ JOHN MORRIS

ARCHITECTS ■ JSA ARCHITECTS   KRANNITZ GEHL ARCHITECTS

LEWIS GRAEBER III & ASSOCIATES   LLOYD & ASSOCIATES ARCHITECTS

LOCATI ARCHITECTS ■ LOONEY RICKS KISS ARCHITECTS ■ MCCORMACK + ETTEN ARCHITECTS ■ MCLAUGHLIN & ASSOCIATES

ARCHITECTS ■ MRJ ARCHITECTS ■ OUTERBRIDGE MORGAN ARCHITECTURE & SPACE PLANNING ■ PFVS-PORTMAN

FRUCHTMAN VINSON SUNDERLAND ARCHITECTS ■ RICHARD M. COLE & ASSOCIATES ARCHITECTS ■ ROBINETTE ARCHITECTS

ROGER BARTELS ARCHITECTS ■ RUDI FISHER ARCHITECTS ■ SCHEURER ARCHITECTS ■ SHAMBURGER DESIGN STUDIO ■ SMUCKLER

ARCHITECTS ■ SPENCER ARCHITECTS ■ STEVEN R. GRAVES ARCHITECTS ■ TMS ARCHITECTS ■ WEST CARROLL ARCHITECTURE

LEADING

RESIDENTIAL

ARCHITECTS

LEADING
RESIDENTIAL
ARCHITECTS

A home is more than a matter of five bedrooms, six baths and his-and-her closets. A house can—and should—be a work of art, one in which the proportions and rhythms of daily life come into play, along with aesthetics and craft. It is one thing to quantify what goes into a house (the square footage, ceiling heights, number of rooms) and another to make it a place for the human psyche and human soul. An architect can do just that.

THE PERFECT
HOME

TABLE OF CONTENTS

TABLE OF CONTENTS

The Perfect Home Leading Residential Architects™ is a
registered trademark of Sandow Media Corporation. ©2005
All rights reserved.

Library of Congress Catalog Card Number: 2004118099

ISBN: 0-9764713-1-0

First Printing: May, 2005

10 9 8 7 6 5 4 3 2 1

Printed in China

FRONT COVER: DesRosiers Architects; Photography: Rauth
Photographic BACK COVER: (UPPER LEFT) Architect: Scheurer
Architects; Photography: Eric Figge Photography (LOWER LEFT)
Architect: DesRosiers Architects; Photography: Laszlo Rego
(UPPER RIGHT) Architect: Krannitz Gehl Architects; Photography:
Bighorn Golf Club (LOWER RIGHT) Architect: Lewis Graeber III &
Associates; Photography: Harold Head

PUBLISHER   Michael J. Ruskin
CREATIVE DIRECTOR   Yolanda E. Yoh
MANAGING EDITOR   Pamela Lerner Jaccarino

PRODUCTION MANAGER   Jody Scalla
PRODUCTION DESIGNER   Andrew Kemp

CONTRIBUTING EDITORS   Al Alschuler, Beth Dunlop,
AND WRITERS   Sarah Greaves Gabbadon, Deborah Hauss,
                                  Paige Loren Herman, H. Susan Mann

Sandow Media Corporation is a cutting-edge publishing company built
around a single philosophy: always exceeding expectations. Based in Boca
Raton, Florida, Sandow Media Corporation is defined by an unrelenting
drive toward quality and innovation. Founded in 2001 by Adam I. Sandow,
Sandow Media specializes in developing consumer books and magazines
in the categories of travel, shelter and beauty. Sandow Media builds
uniquely positioned publications that thrive both in print and online.
Creativity is at the core of every segment of its business and is evident in
all its products and brands.

SANDOW | MEDIA™
Always Exceeding Expectations

CORPORATE HEADQUARTERS
3731 NW 8TH AVENUE
BOCA RATON, FLORIDA 33431
TELEPHONE 561.750.0151 FAX 561.750.0152
WEB www.sandowmedia.com

PRESIDENT AND CHIEF EXECUTIVE OFFICER Adam I. Sandow
CHIEF OPERATIONS AND FINANCIAL OFFICER Scott R. Yablon
CORPORATE EDITORIAL AND CREATIVE DIRECTOR Yolanda E. Yoh
EXECUTIVE VICE PRESIDENT Erik I. Herz
VICE PRESIDENT OF SALES/GROUP PUBLISHER Michael J. Ruskin
VICE PRESIDENT OF OPERATIONS Lloyd Gilick
MANAGING EDITOR Pamela Lerner Jaccarino
GROUP PUBLISHER (LUXE™ PUBLICATIONS) Dana L. Meacham
REGIONAL PUBLISHERS Marianne Feher, Linda G. Frank, Anne Kole, Sal Pandolfo
ADMINISTRATION Shirley M. Costa, Eric Fields, Maritza Severino
GENERAL COUNSEL Boies, Schiller and Flexner; Michael Kosnitzky Esq., Keith Blum, Esq.

Everyone imagines a house at one time or another—from the first stacking of childhood wooden blocks to the elaborate imaginings of pencil on paper. Houses, beautiful houses, are the stuff that dreams are made of. In this book, those dreams become realities with examples of fine architecture across the country, the best works of architects carefully culled to show what a difference design makes.

The houses here come from architects whose work represents various regions of the United States. They do not offer a singular point of view but instead embody a range of architectural thinking. Most of the houses invoke the past in some way—be it the distant past of the Italian Renaissance or the antebellum American South, or a more recent past of the Midwest-bred Prairie School of architecture or the early Modernist period. Some of the houses sprawl through countryside settings, while others fit neatly into urban lots. Most of them are distinctly regional—the New England houses invoking the American Shingle Style, the Western houses echoing the Craftsman tradition.

We are not a nation self-conscious about our history, yet architectural traditions abound here—east and west, north and south. Too often we dismiss our historic architecture as "borrowed" from the English, French, Italian and more, but that is really not the case. There is a rich legacy to draw from, with houses lavish and modest alike. The houses in this book are new, but they celebrate the panorama of our history, interpreting and adapting it as needed. These are houses—be they large or small, brick or wood, stucco or stone—that reflect this rich history but do so in a way that meets modern needs and contemporary lives. Our houses are the building blocks of society. They are the expressions of our hopes and dreams and aspirations. They are an expression of a common aesthetic and of the premium we place—at least some of the time, and one would wish more—on architectural beauty. Houses build neighborhoods, and neighborhoods build communities. Communities, in turn, build societies. It is no exaggeration to say that every house bears that burden or, to put it more optimistically, can embrace that opportunity. That is the mandate at the largest scale.

The German poet Johann Wolfgang von Goethe once said that architecture is "frozen music," and that phrase resonates still. To carry the literary metaphor further, our houses are the instruments to make such music. Each has a solo role and a mission much greater in the larger scheme. Separately, they can be art; together, they can be masterpieces. That is culture. But if houses are culture, they are also comfort. They shelter us, nurture us, offering us a retreat from the rigors of daily life, and keep us safe from harm. Our houses are intensely personal in that they articulate our aspirations and hold our memories. At this level, they are intimate expressions of our identity, and thus we place a premium on them. Some of the ways in which houses express this can be obvious, but there are other ways that are subtler, as repositories of family traditions, as keepers of memories.

Of course, there's function to consider. Obviously, we want our houses to be useful—and usable—but there is more. Houses at their best show us (as individuals, families, a society) at our best. Houses are art, and they are craft.

"Machinery, materials and men—yes—these are the stuffs by means of which the so-called American architect will get his architecture," wrote the greatest of all American architects, Frank Lloyd Wright. "Only by the strength of his spirit's grasp upon all three—machinery, materials and men—will the architect be able so to build that his work may be worthy of the great name architecture."

Trace the house back through history and you will encounter the writings of the first-century BC Roman architect Marcus Vitruvius Pollio, whose words have motivated generations of architects to understand the past and seek out the best, and it is a work that stands today more than two thousand years later. Vitruvius exhorted us to follow the "first principles" of architecture—most often translated as "firmness, commodity and delight." Those principles hold true today when we think about houses: We want them to sit solidly on the ground, and have a substance to them and a capacity to thrill us in ways that are both obvious and subtle.

The history of the Western world is marked by storied architecture—castles, palaces, villas and chateaux that even today evoke our greatest awe and admiration. Elsewhere, Mughal monarchs and Byzantine emperors, among others, were building in styles less familiar but no less breathtaking; the history of the great house is in no way a narrative that takes place only in the Western world. Yet in this "new world," at least in the earliest years of American history, our houses were seldom so formidable. The first settlers who came to Massachusetts and Virginia, and later to other places in the mid-Atlantic and New England seacoasts, found harsh conditions, thus their houses were kept simple; they were modest dwelling places of clapboard or occasionally stone. There are exceptions of course. By the early 19th century, there were the antebellum mansions of the South, followed by the great houses of the Hudson River Valley, among others. But Americans tended to live modestly in the early years of this land. "Yet, European splendor was still tempting to many Americans," says Gwendolyn Wright, professor of architecture at Columbia University's Graduate School of Architecture. Wright notes that by the early 1800s, there were a few examples of "stately residential architecture on a scale of size and grandeur found along the avenues of London or Paris."

Today, those models of early architectural splendor are icons of American luxury—museums and historic sites to marvel at. We seek them out, traveling the Natchez Trace or Louisiana's low country to see plantations, or visiting the houses of our early presidents and patriots—George Washington's Mount Vernon, Thomas Jefferson's Monticello, James Madison's Montpelier. We tour the Berkshires and Newport to see the summerhouses of the Gilded Age, homes of the robber barons, the industrial elite, and much more. We drive the streets of tree-shaded suburbs—Shaker Heights, Ohio, or Lake Forest, Illinois—or peer behind the hedgerows in Palm Beach or Southampton to glimpse the grand houses there.

By the latter half of the 19th century, Americans were building in earnest, establishing architectural traditions that were very much our own and today much admired—from the Shingle Style to Spanish Colonial Revival (ours, yes, and like the Florida rendition which we call Mediterranean Revival, ultimately quite American) to the low-slung modern houses of the Prairie School and beyond. The literature recording our architecture—from professional journals to books to women's magazines and newspapers—show us the country's growing fascination with domestic architecture and the burgeoning debates over form and style, design and decoration.

The array of houses on display in this book ranges in size from modest to grand. The houses are linked by the diligence of their designs and the felicity of their execution. We live in a time of enormous growth and expansion—though it varies year by year, the housing stock grows by at least a million new residences annually—and in a time where we build fast and furiously. Today, one can buy and download a house plan (even for a multimillion-dollar mansion) from the Internet, or snatch up the blueprints for a replica of Monticello. In many places and cases, one can create a house the way children make Mr. Potato Head—an arch here, a vault there, a pediment up top and Palladian windows all around. All this makes the work shown in The Perfect Home series of books ever more crucial, ever more notable.

Architecture is both art and craft. A good house requires an understanding of scale and proportion, of construction and detail. A good house may be simplicity itself or it may be elaborate. But behind its design is a breadth of knowledge, a quest for perfection that comes out of the education of our architects.

Why use the services of an architect? Because an architect has the education, training and experience to artistically interpret what a client desires. An architect collaborates and orchestrates the building of a home from concept to reality, bringing flair, imagination, style and value.

A home is more than a matter of five bedrooms, six baths and his-and-her closets. A house can—and should—be a work of art, one in which the proportions and rhythms of daily life come into play, along with aesthetics and craft. It is one thing to quantify what goes into a house (the square footage, ceiling heights, number of rooms) and another to make it a place for the human psyche and human soul. An architect can do just that.

Beth Dunlop

BARGANIER DAVIS SIMS ARCHITECTS

alabama

Quality architectural design, exceptional professional service and unsurpassed technical expertise are hallmarks of Barganier Davis Sims. Established in 1974, the firm's design philosophy is based on the belief that a residence should reflect the personality and needs of its owners and enhance the features of the surrounding environment. Accordingly, BDS has accumulated numerous local, state, regional and national awards along the way. The firm provides comprehensive services such as master planning and urban design, historic preservation and renovation, interior design and landscape architecture. Its designs are aesthetically pleasing and comparatively low in cost—whether a single-family home, an apartment complex or an institutional, cultural or commercial structure. Other BDS services, also enhanced by state-of-the-art technology, include construction administration and project management, cost containment, schedule control, and quality assurance.

This 9,000-square-foot Montgomery, Alabama residence, flanked by a forest of pine and oak trees, exhibits French country style.

IN HARMONY WITH NATURE

DEEP-SET GREEK-STYLED MOLDING, DORIC COLUMNS AND A
GRACEFUL STAIRWAY PROVIDE ABUNDANT ARCHITECTURAL INTEREST
TO THIS FOYER.

ELABORATE MOLDINGS AND EIGHTEENTH-CENTURY ANTIQUES ADD REFINED
ELEGANCE TO THE FORMAL SALON.

HEAVILY DISTRESSED HEART PINE AND THE LIBERAL USE OF BRICK
AND TILE ADD WARMTH TO A RUSTIC COUNTRY KITCHEN.

ANTIQUE BRICK, SLATE ROOFING, SOARING CHIMNEYS, AND A TRIO OF
DORMER WINDOWS MAKE A STANDOUT OF THIS 9,500-SQUARE-FOOT LOW
COUNTRY STYLE HOME IN LOUISIANA.

Reclaimed wood and brick combine to make a spacious gallery a welcoming one. WARM WELCOME

SOOTHING SYMMETRY | *Imposing painted brick columns frame the succession of French doors in this Montgomery, Alabama home.*

MODERN ART AND AN EXTENSIVE FLORA DANICA CHINA COLLECTION
ADD COLOR AND LIGHT TO A FORMAL SETTING.

FLOOR-TO-CEILING WINDOWS BRING QUIET DRAMA TO A PERSONAL SANCTUARY.

BLACK + WHITE STUDIO ARCHITECTS

alaska

Searching for the "spirit" of a given site and taking into account the many ways in which modern families actually use their homes are some of Black + White Studio's first considerations when designing a residence. "We like to explore many different design ideas for a family and spend a great deal of time at the design stage," says principal Bruce Williams. While recognizing the importance of architectural history and tradition, the firm would say its strong suit is the use of a clear design language to create homes that are current with today's technology and lifestyles. Always respectful of the individual personality of its clients and the features of the site, the firm is known for creating bold and courageous residential designs that add to the occupants' quality of life and enhance their appreciation for the natural beauty of the Alaskan landscape.

Stone, glass and wood are generously used in this open and inviting Alaskan home. FOREST RETREAT

NATURAL ELEMENTS *The sculpted limestone fireplace rises from the floor, separating the great room and the dining area.*

EXPOSED STEEL SUPPORT BEAMS ARE AN ARCHITECTURAL ELEMENT.

EVERY ROOM HAS A SPECTACULAR VIEW OF THE NATURE BEYOND IT.

The flying canopy over the entrance to this 6,000-square-foot contemporary home lends an artistic air.

ROBINETTE ARCHITECTS

arizona

Even though Ron Robinette's work is primarily located in the southwestern environment of Arizona, it captures many styles, from contemporary to Old World traditional. Thoughtfully designed and well-detailed, the houses that the firm creates are often winter homes for part-time residents drawn to the beauty of the Sonoran desert landscape. Accordingly, Robinette places a premium on responding to the demands of desert conditions, and designs homes that seem to rise up right from the Southwest's sandy soil. Materials of concrete or masonry, plaster and copper not only beautify the structure but help protect it from extreme desert climates. Much attention is paid to exterior living spaces and the expansion of interior spaces into the outdoors for year-round use. Quality of construction, sculptural design and the harmony of living both indoors and outdoors are hallmarks of the firm's work. Robinette's hands-on approach, working with clients from start to finish, fosters strong bonds that often turn into lifelong friendships. It's not unusual for Robinette to be asked to create plans for his clients' children, crafting a second generation of homes.

Asian elements blend into this Tucson, Arizona home, whose 4,800-square-foot material palette includes distinctive cast-concrete panels, steel and copper slate.

EAST MEETS WEST

roof tile in a chinked pattern.

THE FLAGSTONE-PAVED PATIO OFFERS A SPECTACULAR VIEW OF TUCSON'S CITY LIGHTS.

AT THE ENTRANCE TO THIS HOME, A CONTEMPORARY COURTYARD COMPRISED OF STONE AND
CONCRETE IMPARTS A SENSE OF CONTAINMENT WHILE ALLOWING FOR A PANORAMIC VIEW.

The faux-finished plaster walls of this impressive gallery show off the owner's art to its best advantage.

A contemporary 4,800-square-foot residence melds into its high desert surround.

A SENSUOUSLY UNDULATING LIGHT TRAY BATHES THE CEILING IN LIGHT WHILE FLOOR-TO-CEILING WINDOWS BLUR THE DISTINCTION BETWEEN INTERIOR AND EXTERIOR LIVING SPACES.

SCHEURER ARCHITECTS

california

The work of Scheurer Architects stands at the vanguard of distinctive residential and community architecture. Created by Mark R. Scheurer AIA, his firm is internationally recognized as a leader in the design of luxury residences, vacation homes and large-scale planned communities. The approach toward a variety of architectural styles responding to individual context has resulted in a multitude of awards and accolades. The firm adheres to a design philosophy of "integration," where the overall scale and exterior massing of the home is evolving simultaneously with the development of the interior floor plan. "Using a more historical vocabulary of architecture combined with unique plan ideas responds more completely to both surroundings as well as its occupants." Scheurer's firm has completed a collection of trendsetting projects and homes that explore traditional vernaculars of architecture in spirited new ways. Unusual courtyards and indoor/outdoor room relationships that introduce light are examples of enduring design ideas that are consistently adapted into the work. Scheurer believes strongly that homes should have an "appropriateness" to his clients and the location and that fully integrated design, landscape and interiors are the ways to achieve this idea.

A series of unfolding architectural experiences characterize this elegant ranch property located in Colorado.

The rustic main entry door opens into an animated Mediterranean style courtyard.

VINTAGE CRAFTSMAN DETAILING IS USED TO CREATE THIS GRACEFUL TRADITIONAL RESIDENCE.

THE DINING ROOM AND KITCHEN COMBINE FOR INFORMAL GATHERING.

THE LUXURY BATH REVEALS FINE ATTENTION TO DETAIL.

COMFORTABLE EXTERIORS COMPLEMENT THE COASTAL SETTING.

BRICK AND WOOD BRING TEXTURE AND WARMTH TO THE LIVING ROOM.

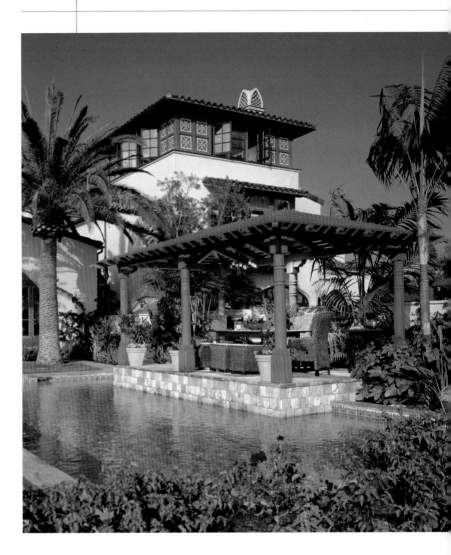

INTIMATE DINING AREA CONTRASTS OPEN SPACES.

RUDI FISHER ARCHITECTS

colorado

Understanding and interpreting classic mountain lifestyle in architectural form are hallmarks of Rudi Fisher Architects. For more than twenty-seven years, this talented boutique firm has designed high-end custom homes and resort projects in and around the Vail Valley. With the Rocky Mountains as a backdrop and starting point, Rudi Fisher Architects creates residences that enhance sites and capture breathtaking views. Honesty of design, harmony, comfort and timelessness are characteristic of the firm's work. The team at Rudi Fisher Architects understands that, for the owners, the home will represent their heart's journey and be a place of social exchanges, family gatherings and moments of solitude. The spaces designed and the materials selected flow from a creative collaboration that gives form to clients' dreams. The firm brings its honesty, integrity and a team approach to each job, with the goal of making clients feel as comfortable as possible through every step of the process.

Warm interior palettes create an inviting, comfortable retreat.

A STUNNING EXAMPLE OF CLASSIC MOUNTAIN ARCHITECTURE.

Expansive windows capture the ever-changing beauty of the horizon.

FRAMING THE VIEW

MUSIC WILL FILL THIS GRAND ENTRY HALL.

The natural beauty of a private family gathering area.

ROGER BARTELS ARCHITECTS

connecticut

Roger Bartels Architects enjoys a well-earned reputation as a leader in exceptional private residences and public domains. Led by principals Roger Bartels and Chris Pagliaro, the firm maintains a guiding philosophy that practicing architecture as if it were a performing art leads to client satisfaction. Bartels' designs are recognized as especially livable environments reflecting a client's individual lifestyle and enhancing it to its utmost potential. The firm's design capabilities are deeply rooted in New England tradition and incorporate the American Shingle style. Regarded for its waterfront residences, the firm produces creations that take full advantage of waterside life, splendid panoramas and proximity to the allure of the outdoors. Roger Bartels Architects view themselves as creative and performance artists, bringing the concept of Gesamtkunstwerk, or "total work of art," to each project. In all its work, the firm strives to create monuments of timeless beauty and lasting utility that contribute to the quality and subtle nuances of the local landscape.

WATERFRONT ELEMENTS CONVERGE OUTSIDE THIS
WESTPORT, CONNECTICUT HOME.

TRADITIONAL MATERIALS AND FIXTURES MAKE THEIR WAY TO A MODERN SETTING.

BRIDGES, MARSH AND CARMO

florida

The principals at Bridges, Marsh and Carmo believe that good design is based on proper proportion, balance and scale. The firm achieves all three in its portfolio of award-winning residential and commercial work. Official architects for the tony Town of Palm Beach, the firm prides itself on attention to even the smallest of details. With offices in Palm Beach and Delray Beach, BMC is a traditional architectural practice dedicated to pleasing the client. The firm realizes the clients' vision while staying true to the rigorous discipline of any given architectural style, from Colonial to contemporary, including restorations. A healthy respect for detailing, placement and structure, and the appropriate use of materials, serve to distinguish the company within its field. Wherever possible, the firm provides contract administration, closely monitoring work during the building process with a regular on-site presence to resolve inevitable construction challenges the moment they occur.

Mediterranean elements and textures create timeless architecture. TUSCAN CLASSIC

Proportion is used to translate eclectic style into a livable human scale.

A CLASSIC LOGGIA INFORMALLY LINKS THE ARRIVAL AREA
TO THE RESIDENCE'S ENTRY.

THE INTRIGUING PORTICO GREETS WELCOME VISITORS.

TERRACES AND VERANDAS OFFER MAGNIFICENT VIEWS ACROSS THE GARDEN
AND POOL TO THE INTRACOASTAL WATERWAY.

HARDSCAPE AND LANDSCAPE ADD TO THE AMBIANCE OF AN ESTATE IN HARMONY WITH ITS SURROUNDINGS.

PFVS ARCHITECTS

georgia

Best known for their work on hotel-related projects, the eighteen-member award-winning team at PFVS Architects is also accomplished in the design of custom single-family estate homes. The firm has designed residences for industry leaders, several professional baseball players and boxer Evander Holyfield, for whom they created a handsome 55,000-square-foot home. PFVS takes pride in delivering a high level of design while simultaneously respecting the boundaries of budget— which is the foundation upon which the company's seventeen-year reputation for architectural creativity and skill rests. Partner Greg Portman says that with every project the practice undertakes, the goal is always to provide a contextually appropriate design that caters to the clients' wish list and to the prevailing environmental factors in an aesthetically pleasing manner. "We deliver exceptional buildings at extraordinary values," says Portman, whose practice has had its work featured in numerous architectural publications. "The most important thing for us," he says, "is to meet or exceed our client's expectations."

This magnificent 55,000-square-foot authentic stucco and limestone home near Atlanta is inspired by Neoclassical and Italian Renaissance styles.

IMPRESSIVE ESTATE

HANDCRAFTED WROUGHT IRON BANISTERS CAPPED WITH
MAHOGANY HANDRAILS EMBELLISH THE ENTRY'S ROTUNDA.

THE HOME'S FLOORING IS CRAFTED FROM FRENCH-POLISHED
LIMESTONE AND OAK WOOD INLAID WITH CHERRY.

Traditional forms and transitional style combine for a refined, 8,500-square-foot, English-inspired Atlanta residence. **GEORGIAN WELCOME**

SPENCER ARCHITECTS

hawaii

One could say that the approach to architectural design by Spencer Architects is almost spiritual. The firm shows a special respect for the land where its projects are built. "We literally 'listen' to the land and strive to place an appropriate building on it—one that meets its needs as much as the client requirements," says principal Spencer Leineweber. Specializing in residential and historic preservation projects, the Hawaiian practice has been recognized nationally for its work by the American Institute of Architects and the National Trust for Historic Preservation and counts the National Park Service as one of its clients. While the firm's architectural signature is as varied as the landscape and as individual as its clients, its 26-year-old reputation is built on working one-on-one with clients, giving them the focused and personal attention a boutique practice is able to deliver. "The foundation of good design begins with attentive listening and close collaboration between architect, owner and contractor," Leineweber says. "It's what allows us to create buildings that respect the uniquely collective way in which Hawaiians live."

A native hau tree provides comfortable shade to an oceanside Diamond Head residence, while a double pitched roof is reminiscent of early post-contact Hawaiian structures.

TRANQUIL BEAUTY

CURVE APPEAL | *A circular cantilevered concrete staircase is dappled in sunlight through a grass shade.*

LARGE SQUARES OF GREEN-STAINED CONCRETE FLOORING, PLASTERED
LAVA ROCK WALLS AND RESAWN TIMBER CEILING RAFTERS ADD ATTRACTIVE
ELEMENTS TO THIS SECOND FLOOR FAMILY LANAI OVERLOOKING THE OCEAN.

HAWAIIAN MOTIFS ARE USED IN THE KAPA DESIGN OF THE DOOR PANELS
AND THE LAUHALA MAT PATTERN OF THE PLASTER CEILING ON THIS
COMFORTABLE OCEAN LANAI.

KOA, A NATIVE ISLAND WOOD, IS USED THROUGHOUT
THE INTERIOR OF THIS HISTORIC HOME.

CURVED GLASS WINDOWS EDGE THE LANAI
OF THE QUEEN ANNE STYLE TURRET.

This historic bed and breakfast on Reed's Island, Hilo, Island of Hawaii, has been in the same family since its construction in 1899.

MCLAUGHLIN & ASSOCIATES

idaho

Buildings designed by McLaughlin & Associates are each creations that respond to the functional and emotional needs of their users. No one style characterizes the firm, which generates architectural and planning solutions that satisfy each client's specific needs after a highly interactive, collaborative process of design, review, revision and redesign. Established in 1975, the full-service firm is renowned for its custom luxury resort, residential and commercial office designs as well as its architectural resort planning. The firm responds not only to clients but also to a structure's surroundings, whether manmade or natural. With its work on display in several states and abroad, McLaughlin & Associates has garnered national and international awards for both design and the use of natural materials.

A timeless marriage of building and landscape.   **PERFECT PROPORTIONS**

Blanket Bay Lodge, one of New Zealand's top-rated luxury hotels.

THE DEEP, WELCOMING PORCH OF A MONTANA HOME.

MULTIPLE WINDOWS ADDRESS NEIGHBORING MOUNTAINS.

This luxurious home sits on an 8,000-acre working cattle ranch in Montana.

BENVENUTI & STEIN

illinois

The driving force behind the success of Benvenuti and Stein is the company's ability to design and build comfortable homes for the way its clientele want to live. Accordingly, each project begins with an in-depth assessment of the client's needs and aspirations. Drawing on attentive listening and interpretive design skills, the firm produces unique living spaces that significantly improve its clients' everyday lives. With capabilities that span the fields of architecture and building, construction management and custom cabinetry, the firm together with its customers benefits from the synergy afforded by a completely integrated approach to design and construction. An experienced team of both conceptual and executive professionals devote themselves to a limited number of jobs each year, ensuring that each project receives meticulous attention to detail. For more than a quarter century, Benvenuti and Stein, located in Evanston, Illinois, has earned high praise from families who live in Chicago and its North Shore communities.

Nestled in a grove of leafy oak trees, the cedar and stucco surfaces of this manor home in Lake Forest embrace the morning sunlight.

NORMANDY MANOR

WORKOUTS SEEM LUXURIOUS IN THIS AT-HOME SPA.

A DRAMATIC ARCHWAY AND PRESERVED GARDEN WALL FRAME CASUAL DINING.

THE CLASSICALLY SCALED FOYER WELCOMES FAMILY AND FRIENDS.

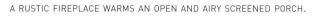

A RUSTIC FIREPLACE WARMS AN OPEN AND AIRY SCREENED PORCH.

UPDATED CLASSIC | *Turn-of-the-century details add charm to a new custom home.*

A COFFERED CEILING DEFINES CASUAL GATHERING SPACES.

ARCHITECTS WELLS KASTNER SCHIPPER

iowa

With origins dating back to 1926, Architects Wells Kastner Schipper is an Iowa-based architecture firm offering a complete range of services, from programming, feasibility studies and master planning through architectural, interior and sustainable design. Nationally recognized for distinctive solutions that meld technology and material with place and precedent, the firm engages in commissions that integrate the principles of sustainable design into a wide range of work that includes governmental, civic, educational, collegiate, long-term healthcare, religious, medical, housing, industrial, and commercial projects. Long before "green" became part of the contemporary lexicon, the firm designed responsible buildings and systems that continue to serve as models of sustainable architecture. Architects Wells Kastner Schipper values its clients as active collaborators in finding solutions consistent with their needs. The firm produces original, yet timeless buildings expressing the people, purpose and place that they are intended to serve. During its long tenure, Architects Wells Kastner Schipper has earned a reputation for innovation and commitment to durability, economic responsibility and timely service.

The transparent lakeside wall of this summer retreat on Lake Okoboji in Northwest Iowa affords gracious views from throughout the home.

THE ENTRANCE IS A SIMPLE, BUT DRAMATIC PORTAL
PLACED WITHIN A PROTECTIVE STONE WALL.

A stream runs through the home, emptying by the window wall into an exterior pond.

FLUID MOTION

THE UPPER LEVEL FLAT OPENS TO THE LOWER LEVEL
WITH SERPENTINE MAHOGANY MILLWORK.

THE DINING ROOM, ON THE EARTH-BERMED MAIN LEVEL.

STEVEN R. GRAVES ARCHITECTS

kentucky

It's all about the site. That's the design philosophy of Steven Graves, principal of a custom residential practice. By trusting the features of the environment to influence a project's final form, the firm creates residences that respect and enhance the landscape on which they are built. Time-honored exteriors suitable to the vernacular of the area—combined with modern interiors that are open, airy and clean—give way to a casual elegance befitting a cosmopolitan community. With the use of columns, ceiling moldings and patterns, and rooms that flow from one to another, he achieves what he calls, "traditional architecture with creative solutions." Graves' ability to listen attentively to clients and to apply creative interpretations to traditional architectural styles, as well as his respect for the elements of symmetry, scale and proportion and use of a palette of mainly natural materials, ensures the realization of the client's dreams. Calling himself the "orchestra leader," he engages his clients, interpreting their goals with skill and sensitivity. The result: a home that its residents will enjoy coming home to year after year.

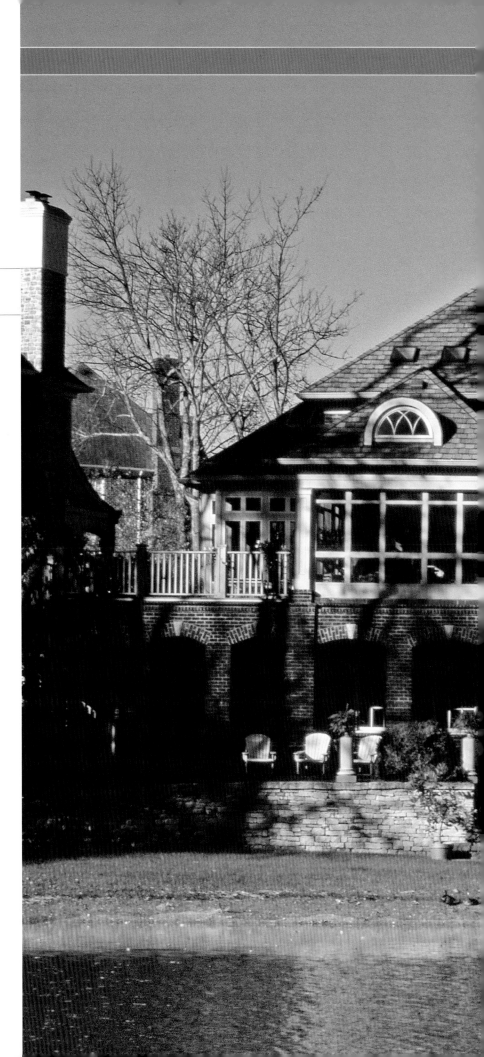

A stately Georgian-inspired clubhouse enjoys a waterfront view of Lexington Reservoir in Kentucky.

NAUTICAL STYLING

The volume of space, spectacular view and design symmetry make this living area a perfect gathering place.

A HOUSE WITH A GOLF COURSE VIEW.

THE LIMESTONE BRICK FIREPLACE IS LAID OUT IN A TRADITIONAL PATTERN.

INDOOR AND OUTDOOR SPACES MERGE, WITH A TREE HOUSE EFFECT.

BARRY FOX ASSOCIATES

louisiana

The team at Barry Fox Architects draws its inspiration from the indigenous 18th- and 19th-century architecture of the South, from traditional regency town homes to Colonial plantation design. Principal Barry Fox is a hands-on designer who is at ease working within the full spectrum of classical design. Fox specializes in Southern Classicism, a distinctive regional style that incorporates Palladian, French, Spanish and Georgian elements. Other distinctively Southern design features, in response to the climatic challenges of sun, rain, heat and light, are deep porches and porticos, which are derivative from the Southern Plantation style. Homes take full advantage of expansive views and the region's brilliant light with the generous use of glass. The firm's collaborative approach extends to the owner's team of interior and landscape designers, with whom they often coordinate, ensuring that the home reflects a common theme and seamless transition between interior and exterior spaces.

The multiple windows and French doors of this Caribbean-Georgian–style home showcase western views of the St. Johns River.

JACKSONVILLE GEORGIAN

This stately Virginia-style brick home is built in the spirit of Thomas Jefferson's architectural achievements and shows a strong Palladian influence.

ONE OF TWO STAIRWELLS THAT MIRROR EACH OTHER ON EITHER SIDE OF THE ATRIUM CENTRAL ROTUNDA, WHICH FORMS THE HEART OF THE HOUSE PLAN.

THE MAIN LIVING ROOM FEATURES FINELY DETAILED MOLDINGS AND A CORNICE WHICH RECALL SIMILAR REFINEMENTS AT JEFFERSON'S MONTICELLO.

A RESTORATION WAS PERFORMED ON THIS LOUISIANA HOME, ORIGINALLY DESIGNED BY HENRY HOWARD, ONE OF THE SOUTH'S LEADING ARCHITECTS OF THE MID-19TH CENTURY.

ENCLOSURE OF THE PORCH WAS PART OF THE RESTORATION OF THIS 19TH-CENTURY GREEK REVIVAL RESIDENCE IN THE GARDEN DISTRICT OF NEW ORLEANS.

The material palette of this Palladian-inspired Atlanta home includes painted brick and a slate roof.   BUCKHEAD IDYLL

A sweeping front arcade and a Mansard roof distinguish this stucco Caribbean plantation-style home, which overlooks the Atlantic on Florida's East Coast.

THIS ENGLISH REGENCY-STYLE RESIDENCE IN NEW ORLEANS REFERENCES THE ELEGANT
TOWN HOMES OF BELGRAVIA SQUARE AND THOSE OF JOHN NASH IN BATH, ENGLAND.

JOHN MORRIS ARCHITECTS

maine

"Successful dreams are always grounded in reality." So says John Morris Architects, a firm that not just designs in harmony with site considerations and the aesthetic sensibilities of clients, but also keeps their budgets in mind. For more than a quarter century, this prominent New England firm has specialized in reinterpreting the vernacular of early 20th-century architecture, developing and executing its designs with great attention to detail and finish. "The pleasure you get from knowing that your dream could be around for generations to come—that will last a lifetime," they say. Each staff member, collectively boasting over seventy years of experience, contributes a distinct perspective and diverse skills using the latest technologies to evolve designs in both two and three dimensions. Morris Construction Services, added to the firm in 1994, offers its clients the additional advantages of in-house construction management, providing single-point responsibility for project delivery through continuous control and close construction coordination, ensuring a smooth transition from vision to reality.

Sweeping rooflines and deep overhangs distinguish this sixteen-room, Shingle-style Maine "cottage," which graces its oceanfront site like a splendid ship.

WATERFRONT ELEVATION

Local fieldstone on the stairwell exterior and entry piers visually anchors the house to the ground.

THE GRACEFUL RED BIRCH AND MAHOGANY STAIRCASE, INFUSED WITH
NATURAL LIGHT, SWEEPS UPWARD TWO STOREYS.

CUSTOM POCKETS IN THE MILLWORK CONCEAL ALL WINDOW TREATMENTS,
ALLOWING UNOBSTRUCTED VIEWS THROUGHOUT THE HOUSE.

CUSTOM-CRAFTED, HAND-RUBBED MAHOGANY MILLWORK
DISTINGUISHES THE LIBRARY.

CANTILEVERED WHITE CEDAR SHINGLE ROOFS WITH WHITE TRIM AND COPPER FLASHINGS
REINFORCE THE ELEGANT HORIZONTAL SWEEP OF THE HOUSE.

BOGGS & PARTNERS ARCHITECTS

maryland

The innovative design and planning solutions of Boggs & Partners Architects have received international acclaim. The award-winning architectural firm brings artistic originality and design excellence to its wide range of corporate, institutional, retail, and residential projects. The firm's portfolio demonstrates a growing, developing body of work that continues to intrigue and impress. Designs encompass a consistency of quality and purpose at a variety of scales. The work itself is characterized by the careful execution of detail, the formal relationship of parts, and the final understanding of form in response to setting. Principal Joseph Boggs FAIA, together with his partners and staff, demonstrates an extraordinary ability to translate strong conceptual approaches into equally compelling architectural forms.

Scale and proportion together with indigenous Maryland stone highlight this 6,500-square-foot modern interpretation of a traditional farmhouse.

A SIMPLE FACADE, YET STRIKINGLY DESIGNED.

COASTAL LOOKOUT   *Curved glass windows, a vertical orientation and the waterfront setting of this 4,000-square-foot Annapolis home give it the feel of a lighthouse.*

THE ENTRANCE IS DEFINED BY ILLUMINATED FORMS AND SHAPES.

AHEARN, SCHOPFER AND ASSOCIATES

massachusetts

"The art of place making" is a unique blend of experience, practicality and vision, according to Ahearn, Schopfer. The firm's core business concentrates on hospitality, entertainment, and retail and residential projects, many of which feature historical characteristics. The firm's extensive expertise translates into solutions that are able to intuitively grasp and anticipate the distinct demands of a project as they relate to the site, program and market. The firm often provides supplemental services such as development master planning, architectural programming, interior architecture documentation, and contract administration. Even though it has been based in Boston for more than a quarter century, the firm's reach is wide, with award-winning architecture and interior design commissions extending from Massachusetts Bay to Manhattan, from Beacon Hill to Boca Raton, and as far west as Santa Barbara, California.

Authentic historical elements and architectural

detail impart character and a sense of importance to this 11,000-square-foot, American Shingle-style gambrel home at Edgartown Harbor on Martha's Vineyard in Massachusetts.

A deep porch, spacious veranda and multiple windows distinguish the 6,500-square-foot shingled summer home.

QUARTER-SAWN RED OAK FLOORING, MAHOGANY COUNTERTOPS
AND PAINTED CUSTOM-CABINETRY MAKE THE KITCHEN THE HEART
OF THIS HOME.

CLEAN LINES, NATURAL LIGHT AND CLASSIC DETAILS PRESERVE THE INTIMACY
AND SERENITY OF THE RECEPTION AREA.

THE CARRIAGE-HOUSE–STYLE GARAGE IS APPOINTED WITH
ARCHITECTURAL ACCENTS.

THE CLASSIC GAMBREL ARCHITECTURE IS REINFORCED WITH
HIGHLY DETAILED LANDSCAPING AND SITE WORK.

An irregular roofline and traditional shuttered windows express the Northwest American/Canadian style of this Osterville, Cape Cod home.

Martha's Vineyard.

A FORMAL SITTING ROOM IS ENLIVENED BY NATURAL LIGHT AND EXPANSIVE HARBOR VIEWS.

DESROSIERS ARCHITECTS

michigan

Artistic form is at the forefront of the exceptional residential, commercial and municipal designs of DesRosiers Architects. Third-generation architect and principal Louis DesRosiers adheres to the philosophy that architecture should strive to create a physical statement rather than simply a structure. The firm's work represents the convergence of three ideals: originality, creativity and excellence. Reflecting its dedication to cutting-edge design, DesRosiers Architects boasts a diversified portfolio of styles and creations from traditional to state of the art. Interiors and exteriors integrate old and new architectural elements to achieve these compelling and innovative designs. Special attention is also given to the design management function as it relates to client communication. All projects are intended to push the limits of design while meeting the individual needs of a client's lifestyle and personality.

POOLSIDE PLEASURE *Illuminated columns are mirrored in the inviting waters of the indoor pool and spa.*

THE HELICAL STAIRCASE SERVES AS A SCULPTURAL CENTERPIECE OF THE ENTRANCE ROTUNDA.

GRAND COLUMNS SUGGEST PAVILIONS OF THE PAST.

The informal gathering room affords breathtaking views of Lake Michigan.   LAKESIDE PANORAMA

RENAISSANCE STYLE   *Reminiscent of a French château, this stately 15,000-square-foot home on Upper Straits Lake, Michigan, exudes an air of mystery and romance.*

AN ELEGANT WHITE BACKDROP SHOWCASES THE PROMINENT CHERRY WOOD AND WROUGHT IRON STAIRCASE.

SMUCKLER ARCHITECTURE

minnesota

Whether the style is contemporary, European, Prairie, or traditional, nationally recognized Smuckler Architecture designs for the specific needs of its clients and their individual lifestyles. Principal Jack Smuckler believes hiring an architect is analogous to commissioning an artist or sculptor to create a one-of-a-kind work of art for a client to live in. The firm that bears his name combines both architectural and construction services for local clients in order to translate its artistic visions into reality. Serving as both architect and builder, he says, eliminates the possibility of a flawed interpretation and results in greater clarity with regard to all details involved, from materials to client communication. For over twenty-five years, Smuckler Architecture has brought a high level of experience, creativity, insight and workmanship to its clients. The firm's collection of residential homes is diverse in style, yet the spaces are all extremely functional to meet client needs. Most important, the homes translate dreams into architectural reality.

This 6,500-square-foot residence on Lake Minnetonka in Minnesota features modern elements and classic lines for a timeless design.

Stone pillars anchor this rustic Minnesota golf course home, accented with Californian clear redwood.

COOL AND SLEEK LIMESTONE FLOORING CONTRASTS WITH THE CURVED GOLD-LEAFED
WALLS OF A MODERN ENTRY.

INTERIOR STONE ACCENTS BRING THE EXTERIOR MATERIALS INSIDE.

Stately stone columns lend architectural weight to the design of this 6,700-square-foot Eden Prairie, Minnesota home.

SEAMLESS TRANSITIONS | *A Lakeville, Minnesota home with a procession of columns and impressive ceiling details divide living, dining and entertaining spaces.*

MULTIPLE LEVELS EXPLOIT THE UNIQUE ELEVATIONS OF THIS 8,000-SQUARE-FOOT BRYANT LAKE, MINNESOTA HOME, CROWNED WITH A SKYLIGHT TO ACCENTUATE THE FOYER.

LEWIS GRAEBER III AND ASSOCIATES

mississippi

The popularity and appeal of the distinctive residential work of Lewis Graeber III and Associates often produces a waiting list for its services. Based on Mr. Graeber's early experience in historic restorations and renovations in New Orleans, his designs draw clients who want unique classic houses with good proportions and details, yet offer livability for modern-day life. Unpretentious, practical and classic are key words in describing the firm's designs. A Graeber-designed house is fully "at home" in the space it occupies, as if it were there for years, seamlessly integrated into its surrounds. Home creations respect the flow of interior spaces and the simplicity of design, and try to give their owners an attractive, comfortable environment for families of all sizes. Drawing on a frank and candid relationship with his clients, Lewis Graeber is able to offer them a tasteful and traditional home that "makes people happy" and which they can enjoy for a lifetime.

SEEN FROM THE BALCONY, THE CEILING OF ANTIQUE OLD HEART PINE AND CYPRESS WOOD AND THE MAGNIFICENT STONE FIREPLACE TAKE CENTER STAGE.

Surrounded by oak and dogwood trees, this spacious hunting lodge in Southern Mississippi is constructed from stained western cedar and stone. MISSISSIPPI ADIRONDACK

An Irish-Georgian front door and a quartet of stone roof finials add interest to this scored-stucco residence in Jackson, Mississippi.

A PALLADIAN WINDOW ALLOWS FULL VIEW OF THE GARDEN BEYOND.

BUILT-IN ARCHITECTURAL DISPLAY CABINETS FRAME
THE ENTRANCE TO AN INTERIOR ROTUNDA.

THE LIBRARY IS INTIMATE, SOPHISTICATED AND MASCULINE.

ALTHOUGH THIS LIVING ROOM IS LARGE AND FORMAL, THOUGHTFUL DESIGN
MAKES IT A WARM, RELAXED AND COMFORTABLE SPACE.

A stone and stucco home on Annandale

BRIGGS ARCHITECTURE + DESIGN

missouri

Briggs Architecture + Design specializes in residential architecture and home design accessories. Beyond designing custom floor plans, exterior forms and interior spaces, the firm is often commissioned to create unique doors, gates, light fixtures, fireplace screens, tools and other home accessories that integrate with the overall architecture. Led by principal Donald G. Briggs AIA, the firm believes that, more than space, what truly defines the character of a house and makes an impression are the details—a beautiful stair railing, well-crafted moldings and attention to light, texture and finely tailored built-ins. Briggs Architecture + Design endeavors to create not only houses, but homes that offer comfort, serenity and security. Each home is designed specifically for the individual family who dwells in it. Committed to direct personal service, the firm designs homes that fulfill the dreams of its clients. These homes continue to nurture and inspire their inhabitants as the years unfold.

This 18,000-square-foot cowboy ranch in southwest Missouri incorporates traditional imagery from the American West.

Leather, reclaimed pine horseshoe trusses and a handsome custom bar combine to create a distinctly masculine space.

THE MASTER SUITE OVERLOOKS A SERENE POOLSIDE VISTA.

BRITISH TUDOR AND CELTIC STYLING LENDS A SENSE OF HISTORY AND CHARACTER TO THIS NEW HOME.

JERRY LOCATI ARCHITECTS

montana

Jerry Locati Architects captures the robust spirit of the New West with progressive designs rendered in timeless natural materials. The signature look of principal Jerry Locati combines wide open spaces and soaring ceilings with a feeling of intimacy and human-scale comfort. To achieve this feel, Locati meticulously joins wood, stone and glass in each of his exquisite custom homes. Bold alpine exteriors, characterized by exposed structural elements, continue inside throughout large expanses of glass-enclosed cozy interior spaces rich in detail. Locati creations are recognized for blending seamlessly with the landscape. This flow between indoors and outdoors epitomizes Western lifestyle and energizes the firm's work. Each home is a direct reflection of its owners and their personalities. Locati Architects collaborates with every client through the length of the building process and beyond, channeling every dream comprehensively and communicating effectively with craftsmen to make them a reality.

Hand-hewn siding and timbers, reclaimed Douglas fir planking, log accents and native stone characterize this 10,000-square-foot home.

MODERN LIFESTYLES FUSE WITH WESTERN TRADITION IN THE MASTER BATHROOM.

NATIVE MATERIALS COMPLEMENT HAND-FORGED IRONWORK.

RECLAIMED FIR FLOORING AND HAND-FORGED IRON DETAILS ADD TO THE HOME'S WARMTH AND LIVABILITY.

MRJ ARCHITECTS

nevada

"We find out what our clients' dreams are, how they live and how they use space," says MRJ principal Mark Johnson. So begins the design process for the small architectural team that is well-practiced in designing for the rigors of a desert environment. Using a palette of hardy natural materials like stone, plaster and clay tile, the designs are mostly wide, open plans where the house can be viewed from front to back. Few interior barriers divide this flow of openness. The liberal use of glass further blurs the lines between indoor and outdoor spaces, fostering an appreciation for the synergy between the two. Rounded walls cascade back to open up the rooms and soften the structure, offering more of a great room conception. Designing form to creatively follow function, the team conceptualizes homes that are comfortable, interesting, energy-efficient and easy to maintain. MRJ's intimate size allows it to develop and maintain relationships with clients for years to come.

The master suite overlooks a lush pool deck designed for outdoor entertaining.

LIGHT FROM THE VENETIAN PLASTER DOME IS REFLECTED ON THE MARBLE FLOOR.

MAHOGANY AND MAPLE WOODS WARM A CONTEMPORARY ENTRYWAY.

5116

THE HORSESHOE SHAPE OF THE BLACK GRANITE BAR ECHOES
THE COFFERED CEILING ABOVE.

THE MUSIC ROOM OFFERS A BREATHTAKING VIEW OF THE LAS VEGAS STRIP.

TMS ARCHITECTS

new hampshire

Buildings that are engineered with excellence, infused with spirit and beauty, linked with their heritage and sensitive to their environment, these are the principles that have guided TMS Architects for more than two decades. Intent on preserving and enhancing a building's environment, the firm provides its exceptional architectural services in three primary areas of work—custom residential, private education/universities, and corporate/commercial. From farmhouse restoration and beachfront residences to cozy cafés and stately banks, TMS Architects is bent on providing warm and inviting spaces with modern functionality. The practice maintains personal and direct contact with clients on each and every project, and the principal responsible maintains involvement with that project from start to finish. Efficient and technologically advanced, with a strong sense of aesthetics and a deep commitment to both the quality and nature of its work, TMS has received numerous AIA awards, New Hampshire Awards of Excellence as well as a coveted Builder's Choice Grand Award.

An impressive seacoast Shingle-style residence on Shapleigh Island in Portsmouth, New Hampshire.

NORTH HAMPTON HAVEN — *A new wing blends seamlessly with the rest of the Greek Revival style in this turn-of-the-century home.*

A GRAND PINE AND MAHOGANY STAIRWAY LEADS TO A STATUESQUE PALLADIAN WINDOW.

THE FIELDSTONE FIREPLACE ASCENT TO THE CEILING IS FLANKED BY
VAULTED DORMER WINDOWS CLAD IN EASTERN PINE.

The natural color palette on the exterior of this 3,000-square foot home allows it to harmonize with the surrounding forest of spruce and hemlock trees.

OUTERBRIDGE MORGAN ARCHITECTURE

new jersey

"Exciting projects attract us," says Outerbridge Morgan Architecture principal Andrew Outerbridge, and it's a sentiment the entire practice of twenty shares. The company philosophy is a simple one: to realize clients' dreams by providing homes of understated yet exceptional elegance. "Our slogan, 'When details count,' means we create an image for our clients," says Peter Morgan, architect and principal of Outerbridge Morgan. Our designs illustrate a sensibility that reflects personal choices, ensuring that each project is fresh. The architects forge a collaborative partnership with their clients, often asking them to collect a portfolio of images that appeal to their personal tastes. The designers then cull and combine these elements, incorporating them into a project that not only has aesthetic appeal but feels right to its residents. With the goal of creating buildings that are sympathetic to the landscape, the company exploits open spaces, light and form to create interiors of simple elegance. Their thoughtful and sensitive designs meld a strong sense of balance, proportion and scale, marrying traditional architecture with playful elements. The firm has been recognized with numerous awards, including, most recently, a New Jersey Award for Historical Preservation for its own offices, near Princeton.

This 7,000-square-foot country manor house in Princeton, New Jersey, features a soaring turret, fieldstone walls, slate roof, and handsome hem-seamed copper trim. **COUNTRY CLASSIC**

RECLAIMED PINE FLOORS AND A HANDMADE LIGHT FIXTURE ACCENT
THIS STRIKING TRANSITIONAL SPACE.

THE GREAT ROOM FEATURES A FIELDSTONE WALL,
HAND-HEWN OAK BEAMS AND CHESTNUT FLOORS.

FRENCH LIMESTONE AND ANTIQUE BEAMS LEND A TRADITIONAL
FEEL TO THIS STATE-OF-THE-ART HORSE BARN.

ANOTHER ATTRACTIVE AND FUNCTIONAL TRANSITIONAL SPACE.

NOTE THE CUSTOM-DESIGNED HANDCRAFTED
HARDWARE ON THE CHESTNUT DOORS.

LLOYD & ASSOCIATES ARCHITECTS

new mexico

Wayne S. Lloyd AIA is president of Lloyd & Associates Architects of Santa Fe, New Mexico. The firm has been providing a variety of architectural services, master planning and interiors, since 1955 for its portfolio that includes fifty-plus residential homes, and mixed-use communities. The mission of Lloyd & Associates is to create enduring, sustainable design respecting the owners aesthetic while maintaining environmental responsibility. Recognized for excellence in design for numerous projects, the firm is steeped in the historical traditions of New Mexican design, sensitive to the spirit and elements of this architecture. Wayne Lloyd continues the founding tradition of Pueblo Revival design, adding a modern vernacular where classic styles and materials are translated to meet the unique needs of each client. Lloyd & Associates recently completed its new office building on Gallery Row in downtown Santa Fe—the first certified LEED (Leadership in Energy & Environmental Design) office building in the city. LEED-certified buildings must adhere to the strict guidelines set by the U.S. Green Building Council.

A 55-foot gallery displays the owners priceless art collection.

CLEAN, LINEAR FEATURES CONTRAST WITH SENSUOUS OBJETS D'ART.

THE FORMAL DINING ROOM INCLUDES A RECESSED-LIT
SHADOW NICHE DISPLAY SHELF.

CREATIVE USE OF ONE-HALF OF A GALVANIZED STEEL DRAINAGE
CULVERT BRINGS DRAMA TO THE CEILING.

CONTEMPORARY SOUTHWESTERN DESIGN IS ENHANCED
WITH INTENSE COLOR IN SYNC WITH NATURE'S HUES.

Pueblo-style elements punctuate with traditional interiors, contemporary furnishings and a structural glass skylight.   **PUEBLO CONTEMPORARY**

BORIS BARANOVICH ARCHITECTS

new york

Its fresh and modern interpretation of classic design is the hallmark of Boris Baranovich Architects. Every project in its portfolio of work, spanning seven states, is designed to respect the landscape and to complement the lifestyles of busy families. Similar to an architectural atelier, BBA works closely with each client, paying special attention to their individual needs and personal style. What results are high-end custom residences that incorporate timeless and traditional elements with a contemporary sensibility. Thorough and meticulous care is taken throughout each stage of the project, but particular emphasis is placed on the interior finishes and detailing that truly make a house a home. The outcome is a residence that provides the perfect architectural solution to the challenges of both landscape and lifestyle.

HAMPTONS DREAM | *Traditional French country and Tuscan styling bring the comforts of home to this seasonal stucco residence.*

THE GRACEFUL SWEEP OF AN ENTRY COLONNADE.

THE ELEGANT COMBINATION OF PAINTED SHINGLE EXTERIORS AND VIRGINIA BRICK.

SHAMBURGER DESIGN STUDIO

north carolina

Shamburger Design Studio brings a sense of history and tradition to its mountain-based, resort-oriented designs. The architectural firm specializes in high-end custom residential creations—located in Cashiers, Hendersonville, Lake Lure and other North Carolina resort areas—and in multifamily and builder-speculative housing. Led by principal Wayland Shamburger, the firm believes that good design is a creative synthesis of client input, site and climate details, and an understanding of structure, materials, space and light. Working from the inside out and in response to the client, the architect develops and nurtures the growth of an idea, the site and surroundings. The completed design is the culmination of the client's dreams and desires. In essence, it is a portrait of the client and results in comfortable spaces that reinforce its owners values. Residences are designed so that clients can settle effortlessly into their retreat, entertain guests, enjoy their families, and allow for a time and place for private moments together.

A rustic mountain home is the centerpiece of this sprawling 50-acre North Carolina estate.

MOUNTAIN ELEGANCE

OUTDOOR SPACES ARE A HIGHLIGHT OF MOUNTAIN LIVING.

An impressive architectural element, the fireplace also serves as the heart of the home.   GATHERING PLACE

TIMBER FRAMING RECALLS BAVARIAN ARCHITECTURE.

WEST CARROLL ARCHITECTURE

ohio

Thorough definition of the design challenge at hand leads to the best design solution, according to West Carroll Architecture. That's why Kevin Carroll spends hours with clients initially, getting to know their personal tastes and architectural dreams. Together they come to a clear, mutual agreement on project goals before the first illustration is drawn. It is Carroll's close-knit relationship with both clients and contractors, and the team of seven's collective personality, that has earned the practice a reputation for delivering a diverse design portfolio. West Carroll's client roster includes residential, commercial and institutional entities. Its work has been recognized with awards from the American Institute of Architects and the Masonry Institute of Northwest Ohio. The practice takes on architectural projects, varying from exhibits at the Toledo Zoo, to the local public television and radio station, to a variety of custom single-family homes. Each construction enhances the flow of activity within the space and has in common a strong sense of movement, structure and light.

A handsome example of traditional Ohio

Traditional joinery methods were used to frame this pool barn with oak king post trussing.

A FORMAL MOTOR COURT ANCHORS THE ENTRANCE TO THE HOME.

THIS LAKESIDE SUNSET PAVILION PROVIDES AN OPEN, YET SHELTERED RECREATIONAL AND GATHERING SPACE THAT CAN BE USED YEAR-ROUND.

TRADITIONAL PRAIRIE STYLE IS WONDERFULLY EXPRESSED IN THIS HILLTOP
NORTHWEST OHIO HOME, NESTLED IN AN OAK GROVE.

Two hundred and sixty degrees of tempered glass frame the light-filled conservatory dining room, enhanced with an Ohio limestone fireplace and stained-oak floor.

ILLUMINATED ELEGANCE

TWIN COPPER CHIMNEYS RISE FROM A CEDAR SHAKE ROOF AND CROWN THIS ENTRANCE PAVILION.

RADIANT-HEATED PORCELAIN FLOOR TILE ALLOWS THIS COVERED PORCH CONNECTING THE REAR OF THE RESIDENCE TO BE USED MOST OF THE YEAR.

ARBOR SOUTH ARCHITECTURE

oregon

Integrity and detail take center stage in the residential and commercial master planning work of Arbor South. Led by principals William A. Randall and Daniel Milton Hill, the award-winning contemporary architectural design firm believes that bringing together all of a project's parts to create an effective "whole" is the essence of architectural integrity. Its goal is to achieve this integrity of design, space and function without compromising or eliminating details. The design process, open to client input, incorporates their ideas and desires. The highly effective and thorough team at Arbor South continually challenge themselves to create imaginative, yet simple solutions to all their architectural design projects. Arbor South's complete architectural services include interior design, structural consultation and project management. No project is too small—the firm brings functional creativity, technical ingenuity and innovative solutions to *all* its clients.

Locally mined broken-top stone is a striking feature of this 4,400-square-foot country manor in Eugene, Oregon.

EDGEWATER HOUSE

SKY MOUNTAIN HOUSE *An eclectic and contemporary interpretation of a Post Modern style.*

THE MAPLE-FLOORED KITCHEN AND GAME ROOM OVERLOOK TWO CITIES.

SLEEK, CONTEMPORARY STYLING.

DISPLAY NICHE SHOWCASING TEXTURED, RAKED PLASTER WALL.

OPEN-BEAM CEILING ACCENTED WITH CHERRYWOOD INSERTS.

DISTINCTIVE CABLE LIGHTING ILLUMINATING
BRAZILIAN CHERRYWOOD FLOOR.

RICHARD M. COLE AND ASSOCIATES

pennsylvania

Twenty-eight years in the business has taught Richard M. Cole many things, most important of which is how to give his clients a sense of sheer delight simply by their living within the spaces he designs. A wealth of experience in building design, restoration and conversion gained over more than five hundred projects, combined with his training as both an engineer and an architect, has yielded a portfolio of outstanding work and a reputation for creativity in commercial, industrial and residential design. Cole spends a tremendous amount of time with each client discussing their needs and desires so that throughout the project there is a clear and mutual understanding of the design goals and nothing is left to the contractor's imagination. The result is a home that is custom-designed to the last square foot, airy and light-filled, and which exploits the beauty of its surroundings.

An English influence is apparent in this 12,000-square-foot Bluebell, Pennsylvania home.

A heated driveway and stone piers with flowers welcome visitors.

FRENCH LIMESTONE FLOORS AND MULTIPLE GLASS DOORS FRAME THIS SERENE POOL HOUSE.

THIS POOL DECK AND GAZEBO MAKE A STRONG DESIGN STATEMENT.

This updated 80-year-old stone mansion in Bryn Mawr, Pennsylvania, retains its classic style.

GEORGIAN BEAUTY

LIGHT FLOODS THROUGH THE THREE FLOORS OF THIS TOWNHOUSE.

CHRISTOPHER ROSE ARCHITECTS

south carolina

The essence of South Carolina's rich traditional architecture is captured in the work of Christopher Rose Architects. The native South Carolinian design team, with principal Christopher Rose at the helm, brings authentic knowledge of the state's architectural history and climatic landscape to its residential designs. The firm approaches its work with an awareness of regional traditions and ever-changing lifestyles, to produce lasting places for people to live in. Christopher Rose Architects follows a common-sense approach to planning and design. Construction methods and materials blend tried-and-true lessons of history with modern techniques. The relationship of rooms to interiors and exteriors maintains simplicity, to create a retreat from busy lives, while details enliven surroundings and appeal to the senses. Christopher Rose Architects designs homes with identities unique to each person and place. Through dialogue and understanding between the client and the architect, the firm creates homes that evoke positive emotions for family and friends.

Handmade brick, tricolor slate roof tiles, twin chimneys, and a turret make this 10,000-square-foot Kiawah Island home in South Carolina, stand out. **ISLAND RETREAT**

An airy, open space is enhanced by bamboo flooring and a majestic bronze fireplace.

FLYING FRONT STEPS AND HORIZONTAL METAL RAILINGS
EVOKE PLANTATION AND MARITIME IMAGERY.

THE COFFERED CEILING GIVES A TRADITIONAL FEEL TO THIS GREAT ROOM.

A turret and sweeping roofline add an interesting composition to this 4,000-square-foot Kiawah Island home.

Classic Tuscan detailing and Italian clay tile bring a European sensibility to this stucco home in Isle of Palms, South Carolina.

VIEWS UNFOLD FROM THE DINING AREA.

LOONEY RICKS KISS ARCHITECTS

tennessee

Quality of life and timeless architectural fundamentals for today's world are hallmarks of the Housing Studio of Looney Ricks Kiss Architects. The firm brings its expertise to architecture, interiors, planning and research in virtually every component of residential and community design. Each design maximizes the day-to-day experience of its user and creates a memorable sense of place that is respectful of its location and surroundings, be they urban or rural. The LRK team has proven success and skill in balancing the formula for quality, quantity and cost of a project, whether it's high-end luxury or more modest. The firm credits its substantial accomplishments to its exceptional awareness of the marketplace and the high level of communication it enjoys with its clients. Offices of Looney Ricks Kiss can be found in Tennessee, Florida and New Jersey. Since its founding in 1983, the firm has completed hundreds of projects throughout the United States, the majority of which are in the South and East. Projects have won wide recognition in various publications and numerous national and regional awards for design excellence.

The traditional detailing and combination of materials completes this stately facade in Eads, Tennessee.   **MAJESTIC ESTATE**

Center hall dining provides for cozy, yet comfortable use.

BUILDING MATERIALS AND COMPONENTS ARE
INTEGRATED INTO THE HOME'S DESIGN.

PROPORTION, DETAILS AND MATERIALS ARE SKILLFULLY APPLIED
FROM FORMAL TO INFORMAL SPACES.

CLASSICAL STYLE WITH FORMAL AND INFORMAL SPACES
RESPECTS THE DOUBLE-FRONTAGE URBAN LOT.

THIS VERNACULAR FACADE DOES NOT FULLY REVEAL
THE MODERN FLOOR PLAN WITHIN.

ENGLISH COTTAGE INFLUENCES PROVIDE A COMFORTABLE SCALE AND CHARACTER.

COLLINS ARCHITECTS

texas

Award-winning Collins Architects and Construction Company, an integrated design and construction studio, offers clients a better building experience. Educated in art, architecture and business at Rice University, Rodney Collins brings both artistic expertise and construction skill to residential design. Through dramatic use of materials, environmental sensibility and attention to client needs, the designs of Collins Architects go beyond mere shelter. They harmonize the homes they create with the natural surroundings, taking full advantage of nature's amenities. The firm challenges itself to make fresh designs while building durable structures that can be passed down through generations. Because of its construction expertise, Collins Architects understands the relative value of materials and their impact on budgets, schedules and quality-of-life issues, and sees itself as particularly well-equipped to draw out the best from a site and the materials at hand, balancing imagination and brick-and-mortar reality. The firm can start clients out by exploring prototypes, then customize to meet their individual needs and desires. The guiding principle is the belief that a home is a beautiful place for growth and learning, and serves as a rich background for life.

This Texas home blends natural elements of wood and stone with metal, blurring the distinction between indoor and outdoor spaces.

SCENE STEALER

Unusual contours coalesce into clean, contemporary lines with organic shapes.

THE SERENITY AND BEAUTY OF AN ENCLOSED JAPANESE-STYLE COURTYARD.

STAINED REDWOOD, STONE AND BLACK STEEL UNITE.

Arching beams survey an earthy mix of natural materials that soften these modern architectural features.

JSA ARCHITECTS

utah

The award-winning designs of JSA Architects span the style spectrum, from French Country to Arts and Crafts to high-concept Contemporary. Each design is carefully customized to the needs of both the client and the landscape and is thoughtfully conceptualized to express the personality of the owners. Accordingly, designs take into account a number of other considerations, including the peculiarities of Utah's topography, which incorporates desert, park land and mountain and snow-capped landscapes. Specializing in high-end resort homes for clients who often live out of the state and visit primarily for recreation, JSA Architects creates homes that can be flung wide open during the warmer months but provide strong defense against harsh winter climes. While attention to detail and appropriateness of design are paramount, maximizing the value of the client's investment is also of great importance to the team of twenty-two architects and interior designers, whose work has been featured in numerous architectural publications. "We strive for a seamless transition between indoor and outdoor spaces," says principal Chris Jensen, "and we ultimately try to make both spaces equally livable for utility year-round."

French Country styling and expansive mountain views make this 8,000-square-foot desert sandstone house a pleasure to come home to.

A COZY SEWING LOFT OVERLOOKS THE FAMILY ROOM AND KITCHEN.

HAND-HEWN DOUGLAS FIR BEAMS FRAME THE LIVING ROOM'S VAULTED CEILINGS.

Utah's Wasatch Mountains make a stunning backdrop for this handsome home.   COLONNADE VISTA

Mountain contemporary and Arts and Crafts elements combine in this 7,500-square-foot Park City, Utah residence.

SOARING WINDOWS OFFER SPECTACULAR VIEWS OF THE WASATCH MOUNTAINS.

ISLAND ARCHITECTS

virginia

Island Architects is known for its award-winning, site-responsive island architecture created for coastal and inland communities throughout the Bahamas, Gulf Coast and Eastern Seaboard. The firm's work extends to single- and multifamily residences and to commercial property. Led by G.M. (Skip) Wallace Jr., AIA, the practice reflects his affinity for resort architecture, stemming from his Scottish roots. He is the great-grandson of Robert White, a professional golf course architect from St. Andrews who came to America around the turn of the last century and went on to become the first president of the PGA of America, as well as a charter member of the American Society of Golf Architects. Island Architects embraces the design theory that says when natural site amenities shape the form, the rooms seem to locate themselves. Island Architects' creations are characterized by their use of natural light, which the firm considers the most important indigenous feature of any space. The work further captures the appeal of island resort life through a blend of textures, native building materials and muted colors.

A copper roof and hand-dipped cedar shingles protect this 9,000-square-foot Kiawah Island, South Carolina coastal cottage. **ISLAND IDYLL**

GENTLEMAN'S CLUB *This masculine club room's spiral stairway leads to a pine-paneled library and master suite.*

ANTIQUE PINE WAINSCOTING AND PORCELAIN FIXTURES LEND AN OLD WORLD FEEL.

LIGHTHOUSE-SHAPED POSTS PUNCTUATE THE BANISTER.

ELEGANT GRANITE COUNTERTOPS ARE JUXTAPOSED WITH A RUSTIC
BUTCHER-BLOCK ISLAND

COASTAL CHARISMA | *An outdoor fireplace and island-inspired furnishings provide all the comforts of home.*

AN INFINITY-EDGE POOL AND HOT TUB GIVE AN OUTDOOR OASIS JUST THE RIGHT SPLASH.

KRANNITZ GEHL ARCHITECTS

washington

More than any signature style or particular expression, creative flexibility marks the firm of Krannitz Gehl Architects. Each design springs from the unique qualities of the specific site, combined with careful attention to the personal requirements and dreams of the individual client. The firm's philosophy is that the process is integral to the final design: In active collaboration with the client, the team balances need with desire, context with culture, and concept with detail. Principals Bryan Krannitz and Barry Gehl take the lead in fostering an open exchange, encouraging discovery and pursuing diversity—from architectural styles to unusual materials. Rather than viewing budget and program as constraints, the firm uses these parameters to launch innovative explorations. Ultimately, their creative solutions transcend expectations, presenting clients with livable spaces that gracefully dissolve the boundaries between enclosure and landscape. The elegant designs satisfy and excite, lifting the spirits and inspiring the senses.

Common floor and wall materials both inside and out make the transition between interior and exterior spaces truly seem to disappear.

THE MASTER BEDROOM LANDING, AS SEEN FROM THE STAIR TOWER.

THE HOME IS WELL SITED TO TAKE IN THE EXPANSIVE VIEW.

DEEP ROOF OVERHANGS EXTEND THE INTERIOR LIVING
SPACES TO THE OUTDOORS.

THE RESIDENCE SEEMS TO HAVE RISEN OUT OF ITS SITE.

MCCORMACK + ETTEN ARCHITECTS

wisconsin

Quality design can only be achieved by creativity, hard work and good taste, and ultimately the success of a design solution can only be measured relative to a client's needs. This formula has been the founding principle of McCormack + Etten Architects, resulting in a varied portfolio of custom homes. From the firm's inception, Ron McCormack and Ken Etten set out to form a boutique-style professional office, one that would maintain a high level of personal service for its clientele. Founded in 1992, the practice remains a "hands-on" firm, still structured to deliver the personal attention of its partners and staff. M + E takes pride in its creative design sense, its comprehensive technical knowledge and its clear understanding of the architect's role in the construction industry. The firm combines traditional design in a variety of styles with contemporary planning concepts that complement clients' lifestyles. Pragmatic planning leads to creativity and back again, bringing fresh and exciting solutions that will withstand the test of time and satisfy client needs.

A quartet of finials crown this formal French manor house–style residence on the shores of Geneva Lake in Williams Bay, Wisconsin.

Surrounded by spruce and maple trees, this stunning Craftsman home is in the lakeside resort community of Lake Geneva, Wisconsin.

AN INVITING ENTRY PORCH OFFERS VIEWS OF GENEVA LAKE.

A WHITE OAK CEILING AND FLOOR AND STRIKING RUMFORD FIREPLACE BRING
WARMTH TO THIS OPEN AND INVITING BREAKFAST ROOM.

THE INVITING INTERIOR OF THE DINING ROOM IS CONSISTENT WITH THE CRAFTSMAN STYLING OF THE HOME.

ELLIS NUNN & ASSOCIATES

wyoming

Ellis Nunn & Associates defines Rocky Mountain rustic charm in its high-end log and mountain-style custom homes and commercial properties. The firm is notable for creating expansive spaces with a cozy lodge feel. Intricate multiple rooflines with designs that mimic the steeping ridgelines of surrounding mountain ranges are one of Ellis' trademark styles, as are open floor plans with large picture windows that maximize panoramic vistas. By using large fixed glass and true divided light operating windows, Ellis captures surrounding views from every room. Design creativity is essential to Ellis Nunn & Associates. Equally as important is client service. Ellis spends a considerable amount of time discussing clients' desires and needs for their home, which helps in producing plans that are specific to individual preferences.

Located at the base of the Hobacks at Jackson Hole Mountain Resort, the exterior of this 6,000-square-foot home features stacked stone, cedar and log.

VIVID VIEWS

LARGE TRUSSES IN THE PORTE COCHERE, ARCHED FRAMING AROUND THE FRONT DOOR AND STACKED STONE WALLS AND PILLAR SUPPORTS CREATE AN IMPRESSIVE ENTRY.

THE HISTORICAL SITE OF THE SLEEPING INDIAN IN THE BRIDGER TETON
NATIONAL FOREST IS IN FULL VIEW THROUGH THE KITCHEN WINDOW
AT THIS GROS VENTRE NORTH SUBDIVISION RESIDENCE.

INDEX

A

AHEARN SCHOPFER AND ASSOCIATES, P.C.
BOSTON OFFICE
160 Commonwealth Avenue
Boston, MA 02116
Ph: 617-266-1710 ■ Fx: 617-266-2276

VINEYARD OFFICE
Nevin Square, 17 Winter Street
Edgartown, MA 02539
Ph: 508-939-9312 ■ Fx: 508-939-9083
Email: info@AhearnSchopfer.com
Website: www.ahearnschopfer.com

ARBOR SOUTH ARCHITECTURE, P.C.
4765 Village Plaza Loop, Suite 200
Eugene, OR 97401
Ph: 541-344-3332 ■ Fx: 541-344-1597
Email: info@arborsouth.com
Website: www.arborsouth.com

**AWKS—ARCHITECTS WELLS
KASTNER SCHIPPER**
1105 Grand Avenue, Suite 200
West Des Moines, IA 50265
Ph: 515-327-0007 ■ Fx: 515-327-0077
Email: studio@a-wks.com
Website: www.a-wks.com

B

**BARGAINER DAVIS SIMS
ARCHITECTS ASSOCIATED**
624 South McDonough Street
Montgomery, AL 36104
Ph: 334-834-2038 ■ Fx: 334-834-1037
Email: sharrison@bdsarch.com
Website: www.bdsarch.com

BARRY FOX ASSOCIATES ARCHITECTS, LTD.
1519 Washington Avenue
New Orleans, LA 70130
Ph: 504-897-6989 ■ Fx: 504-899-4456
Email: barry@barryfox.com

BENVENUTI AND STEIN, INC.
2001 Greenleaf Street
Evanston, IL 60202
Ph: 847-866-6868 ■ Fx: 847-866-8010
Email: ben@benvenutiandstein.com
Website: www.benvenutiandstein.com

BLACK + WHITE STUDIO ARCHITECTS
3400 Spenard Road, Suite 3
Anchorage, AK 99503
Ph: 907-770-5773 ■ Fx: 907-770-5774
Email: info@bwstudioarchitects.com
Website: www.bwstudioarchitects.com

BOGGS & PARTNERS ARCHITECTS
410 Severn Avenue, Suite 406
Annapolis, MD 21403
Ph: 301-858-8118 ■ Fx: 301-858-8421
Email: contact@boggspartners.com
Website: www.boggspartners.com

BORIS BARANOVICH ARCHITECTS
153 Waverly Place, Suite 1200
New York, NY 10014
Ph: 212-627-1150 ■ Fx: 212-645-1389
Email: bbaranovich@borisbaranovicharchitects.com
Website: www.borisbaranovicharchitects.com

BRIDGES, MARSH AND CARMO, INC.
DELRAY BEACH OFFICE
124 Northeast 5th Avenue
Delray Beach, FL 33483
Ph: 561-278-1388 ■ Fx: 561-278-7841
PALM BEACH OFFICE
18 Via Mizner
Palm Beach, FL 33480
Ph: 561-832-1533 ■ Fx: 561-832-1520
Email: dbma@netrox.net

INDEX

BRIGGS ARCHITECTURE + DESIGN
MISSOURI OFFICE
301 West Walnut
Springfield, MO 65806
MONTANA OFFICE
120 South 5th Street, Suite 203
Hamilton, MT 59840
Ph: 406-375-1111 ▪ Fx: 406-363-1414
Email: info@briggsarch.com
Website: www.briggsarch.com

C

CHRISTOPHER ROSE ARCHITECTS, P.A.
3509 Meeks Farm Road
Johns Island, SC 29455
Ph: 843-559-7670 ▪ Fx: 843-559-7673
Email: info@christopherrosearchitects.com
Website: www.christopherrosearchitects.com

COLLINS ARCHITECTS & CONSTRUCTION CO.
1963 Lexington, Number 2
Houston, TX 77098
Ph: 713-522-4220 ▪ Fx: 713-528-3090
Email: rcollins@collinsarchitects.com
Website: www.collinsarchitects.com

D

DESROSIERS ARCHITECTS
36330 Woodward Avenue, Suite 100
Bloomfield Hills, MI 48304
Ph: 248-642-7771 ▪ Fx: 248-642-3147
Email: mail@desarch.com
Website: www.desarch.com

E

ELLIS NUNN & ASSOCIATES
70 North Center Street
Jackson, WY 83001
Ph: 307-733-1779 ▪ Fx: 307-733-6909
Email: Sharon@ellisnunnarchitects.com
Website: www.ellisnunnarchitects.com

I

ISLAND ARCHITECTS
11800 Chester Village Drive, Suite D
Chester, VA 23831
Ph: 804-768-8810 ▪ Fx: 804-768-0343
Email: info@islandarchitects.com
Website: www.islandarchitects.com

J

JOHN MORRIS ARCHITECTS
49 Mechanic Street
Camden, ME 04843
Ph: 207-236-8321 ▪ Fx: 207-236-6391
Email: info@johnmorrisarchitects.com
Website: www.johnmorrisarchitects.com

JSA ARCHITECTS, LLC
3115 E. Lion Lane, Suite 300
Salt Lake City, UT 84121
Ph: 801-278-8151 ▪ Fx: 801-278-8661
Email: corey.solum@jsa-llc.com
Website: www.jsa-llc.com

K

KRANNITZ GEHL ARCHITECTS
765 N.E. Northlake Way
Seattle, WA 98105
Ph: 206-547-8233 ▪ Fx: 206-547-8219
Email: barry@krannitzgehl.com
Website: www.krannitzgehl.com

L

LEWIS GRAEBER III & ASSOCIATES
2009 London
Jackson, MS 39211
Ph: 601-366-3611 ▪ Fx: 601-366-3641
Email: lagraeber@hotmail.com

LLOYD & ASSOCIATES ARCHITECTS
501 Halona Street
Santa Fe, NM 87501
Ph: 505-988-9789 ▪ Fx: 505-986-1165
Email: info@lloyd-architects.com
Website: www.lloyd-architects.com

LOCATI ARCHITECTS
402 East Main Street, Suite 202
Bozeman, MT 59715
Ph: 406-587-1139 ▪ Fx: 406-587-7369
Email: info@locatiarchitects.com
Website: www.locatiarchitects.com

LOONEY RICKS KISS ARCHITECTS, INC.
MEMPHIS OFFICE
175 Toyota Plaza, Suite 600
Memphis, TN 38103
Ph: 901-521-1440 ▪ Fx: 901-525-2760
Email: info@lrk.com
Website: www.lrk.com

CELEBRATION, FLORIDA OFFICE
610 Sycamore Street, Suite 120
Celebration, FL 34747
Ph: 407-566-2575 ▪ Fx: 407-566-2576
Website: www.lrk.com
Other offices located in Nashville, TN,
Princeton, NJ, and Rosemary Beach, FL

M
MCCORMACK + ETTEN ARCHITECTS
400 Broad Street
Lake Geneva, WI 53147
Ph: 262-248-8391 ▪ Fx: 262-248-8392
Email: contact@mccormacketten.com
Website: www.mccormacketten.com

MCLAUGHLIN & ASSOCIATES
ARCHITECTS CHARTERED, AIA
126 Saddle Road
Ketchum, ID 83340
Ph: 208-726-9392 ▪ Fx: 208-726-9423
Email: gretchen@mclaughlinarchitects.com
Website: www.mclaughlinarchitects.com

MRJ ARCHITECTS
4790 West University Avenue
Las Vegas, NV 89103
Ph: 702-869-3808 ▪ Fx: 702-869-3813
Email: mrjarch@aol.com

O
OUTERBRIDGE MORGAN
ARCHITECTURE & SPACE PLANNING, LLC
10 Princeton Avenue
Rocky Hill, NJ 08553
Ph: 609-466-7796 ▪ Fx: 609-497-3909
Email: info@omarch.net
Website: www.omarch.net

P
PFVS—PORTMAN FRUCHTMAN VINSON
SUNDERLAND ARCHITECTS
5416 Glenridge Drive
Atlanta, GA 30342
Ph: 404-503-5000 ▪ Fx: 404-503-5050
Email: info@pfvsarch.com
Website: www.pfvsarch.com

R
RICHARD M. COLE & ASSOCIATES ARCHITECTS
15 South Third Street
Philadelphia, PA 19106
Ph: 215-922-6930 ▪ Fx: 215-922-4549
Email: architects@rmcoleassoc.com
Website: www.rmcoleassoc.com

ROBINETTE ARCHITECTS, INC.
1670 East River Road, Suite 112
Tucson, AZ 85718
Ph: 520-323-3979 ▪ Fx: 520-888-5518
Email: architects@robinettearchitect.com
Website: www.robinettearchitect.com

ROGER BARTELS ARCHITECTS, LLC
27 Elizabeth Street
South Norwalk, CT 06854
Ph: 203-838-5517 ▪ Fx: 203-838-5616
Email: rba@rogerbartelsarchitects.com
Website: www.rogerbartelsarchitects.com

INDEX

RUDI FISHER ARCHITECTS, INC.
P.O. Box 641
Vail, CO 81658
Ph: 970-949-5624 ■ Fx: 970-949-7775
Email: rfa@rudifisherarchitects.com
Website: www.rudifisherarchitects.com

S

SCHEURER ARCHITECTS
NEWPORT BEACH OFFICE
20411 Southwest Birch Street, Suite 330
Newport Beach, CA 92660
Ph: 949-752-4009 ■ Fx: 949-752-8737

PALM SPRINGS OFFICE
174 North Palm Canyon Drive, Suite 5
Palm Springs, CA 92262
Ph: 760-864-6620 ■ Fx: 760-864-6630
Email: info@scheurerarchitects.com
Website: www.scheurerarchitects.com

SHAMBURGER DESIGN STUDIO
118 Ashwood Road
Hendersonville, NC 28791
Ph: 828-692-2737 ■ Fx: 828-694-0737
Email: designstudio@brinet.com
Website: www.shamburgerdesignstudio.com

SMUCKLER ARCHITECTS, INC.
7509 Washington Avenue South
Edina, MN 55439
Ph: 952-828-1908 ■ Fx: 952-828-6007
Email: jsmuckler@smuckler.com
Website: www.smucklerarchitects.com

SPENCER ARCHITECTS INC.
1810 University Avenue, Suite 101
Honolulu, HI 96822
Ph: 808-955-9595 ■ Fx: 808-944-9115
Email: aspencer@hawaii.edu

STEVEN R. GRAVES ARCHITECTS
2405 Harrodsburg Road
Lexington, KY 40504
Ph: 859-219-3181 ■ Fx: 859-296-4444
Email: srgraves@juno.com

T

TMS ARCHITECTS
1 Cate Street
Portsmouth, NH 03801
Ph: 603-436-4274 ■ Fx: 603-431-1828
Email: info@tms-architects.com
Website: www.tmsarchitects.com

W

WEST CARROLL ARCHITECTURE
5470 South Main Street
Sylvania, OH 43560
Ph: 877-850-0001 ■ Fx: 419-517-1000
Email: kevin.carroll@westcarroll.com
Website: www.westcarroll.com

PHOTO CREDITS

Pages 2-3: Architect: Barry Fox & Associates; Photography: Van Jones Martin **Page 5:** Architect: Scheurer Architects; Photography: Eric Figge Photography **Page 6:** Architect: DesRosiers Architects; Photography: Beth Singer **Page 9:** Architect: Roger Bartels Architects; Photography: John Kane **Page 10:** Architect: Ahearn Schopfer & Associates; Photography: Greg Premru Photography **Page 13:** Architect: Roger Bartels Architects; Photography: John Kane **Page 14:** Architect: Krannitz Gehl Architects; Photography: Benjamin Benschneider **Pages 16-23:** Matt Silk Photographics **Pages 24-29:** Ken Graham Photography **Pages 30-31:** Tim Fuller **Pages 32-33:** Ray Albright **Pages 34-35:** James Yochum **Pages 36-37:** Tim Fuller **Pages 38-45:** Eric Figge Photograhy **Pages 46-47:** Karl Neumann **Pages 48-49:** David O. Marlow **Page 50:** D.R. Edwards **Page 51:** Dann Coffey Photo **Pages 52-56:** John Kane **Page 57:** Ken Smith **Pages 58-63:** Digby Bridges **Page 64:** (LEFT) Digby Bridges **Pages 64-65:** Matt Silk Photographics **Pages 66-69:** Thomas Watkins Photography **Pages 70-71:** Gary Knight & Associates **Pages 72-75:** Franzen Photography **Pages 76-77:** Linny Morris Cunningham **Pages 78-79:** Fred Linholm **Pages 80-81:** Patrick Reynolds **Pages 82-93:** Roger Wade Studio, Inc. **Pages 84-85:** Judy Slagle **Page 86:** (LEFT) Judy Slagle, (RIGHT) James Yochum **Page 87:** (LEFT) Steve Hall Hedrich Blessing, (RIGHT) James Yochum **Pages 88-89:** Paul Schlismann **Pages 90-93:** Timothy Hursley **Pages 94-95:** King Au **Pages 96-103:** Walt Roycraft Photographers **Pages 104-111:** Van Jones Martin **Pages 112-119:** Brian Vanden Brink **Pages 120-121:** Maxwell McKenzie **Pages 122-123:** Celia Pearson **Pages 124-125:** Maxwell McKenzie **Pages 126-133:** Greg Premru Photography **Pages 134-137:** Laszlo Rego **Page 137:** (RIGHT) Beth Singer **Pages 138-139:** Rauth Photographic **Pages 140-141:** George Dzahristos **Page 141:** (RIGHT) George Dzahristos **Pages 144-145:** Jerry Swanson Photography **Pages 146-149:** Landmark Photography & Design **Pages 150-151:** Matt Silk Photographics **Pages 152-157:** Harold Head **Pages 158-159:** Steven Peterson **Pages 160-161:** Patricia Pierce **Pages 162-163:** Timothy Ludwig **Pages 164-171:** Roger Wade Studio, Inc. **Pages 172-179:** Chawla Associates **Pages 180-181:** Cheryle St. Onge **Pages 182-183:** James Salomon **Pages 184-185:** Sandy Agrifiotas **Pages 186-191:** Mike Slack **Pages 192-197:** Jack Parsons **Pages 198-199:** David Anderson **Pages 200-201:** Ron Papageorge **Page 201:** (RIGHT) James Chotas **Page 202:** (LEFT) William Bretzger **Pages 202-203:** Chong B. Tan **Pages 204-209:** Matt Silk Photographics **Page 209:** (RIGHT) Roger Wade Studio, Inc. **Pages 210-213:** Steven Elbert Architectural Photography **Pages 214-215:** David Holman Photography **Pages 216-217:** Steven Elbert Architectural Photography **Pages 218-223:** Gary Tarleton, ASMP **Pages 224-231:** Barry Halkin **Pages 232-233:** John McManus Photography **Pages 234-235:** Creative Sources Photography **Pages 236-237:** David Costopulos **Pages 238-239:** Dickson Dunlap Studios **Pages 240-241:** Terry Sweeney/Sweeny South Commercial Photography **Pages 242-243:** Jeffrey Jacobs/Architectural Photography, Inc. **Page 244:** (LEFT) Robt Ames Cook Photography **Page 245:** Robt Ames Cook Photography **Pages 246-247:** Scaletta Photography **Page 247:** (RIGHT) Scaletta Photography **Pages 248-253:** Paul Hester **Pages 254-259:** Josh Caldwell **Pages 260-267:** Dickson Dunlap Studios **Pages 268-271:** Benjamin Benschneider **Pages 272-273:** Bighorn Golf Club **Pages 274-275:** Ron McCormack **Pages 278-281:** Brian Thomas Photo **Pages 282-283:** Cameron Neilson **Pages 284-287:** Roger Wade Studio, Inc. **Page 286:** (LEFT) David J. Swift **Page 289:** Architect: Locati Architects; Photography: Roger Wade Studio, Inc. **Page 292:** Architect: Roger Bartels Architects; Photography: John Kane **Page 295:** Architect: Robinette Architects; Photography: James Yochum **Page 296:** Architect: Roger Bartels Architects; **Back Cover:** (UPPER LEFT) Architect: Scheurer Architects; Photography: Eric Figge Photography (LOWER LEFT) Architect: DesRosiers Architects; Photography: Laszlo Rego (UPPER RIGHT) Architect: Krannitz Gehl Architects; Photography: Bighorn Golf Club (LOWER RIGHT) Architect: Lewis Graeber III & Associates; Photography: Harold Head

Additional Credits: Pages 158-161: Builder: Ron Middleton **Pages 162-163:** Builder: Michael D. Smith **Pages 210-213:** Interior Design: InterDesign Studio **Pages 210-213:** Builder: Brunbaugh Construction **Pages 214-215:** Builder: The Lathrop Company **Pages 216-217:** Interior Design: InterDesign Studio **Pages 216-217:** Builder: Prete Builders